CHILDHOOD FEARS AND ANXIETIES

PHOBIAS

CHILDHOOD FEARS AND ANXIETIES

PHOBIAS

H.W. POOLE

SERIES CONSULTANT
ANNE S. WALTERS, Ph.D.

Emma Pendleton Bradley Hospital

Warren Alpert Medical School of
Brown University

MASON CREST

Mason Crest
450 Parkway Drive, Suite D
Broomall, PA 19008
www.masoncrest.com

MTM Publishing, Inc.
435 West 23rd Street, #8C
New York, NY 10011
www.mtmpublishing.com

President: Valerie Tomaselli
Vice President, Book Development: Hilary Poole
Designer: Annemarie Redmond
Copyeditor: Peter Jaskowiak
Editorial Assistant: Leigh Eron

Series ISBN: 978-1-4222-3721-2
Hardback ISBN: 978-1-4222-3728-1
E-Book ISBN: 978-1-4222-8061-4

Library of Congress Cataloging-in-Publication Data
Names: Poole, Hilary W., author.
Title: Phobias / by H.W. Poole; series consultant: Anne S. Walters, Ph.D.,
    Emma Pendleton Bradley Hospital, Alpert Medical School/Brown University.
Description: Broomall, PA: Mason Crest, [2018] | Series: Childhood fears and
    anxieties | Audience: Age 12+ | Audience: Grade 7 to 8. | Includes index.
Identifiers: LCCN 2016053122 (print) | LCCN 2016053673 (ebook) | ISBN
    9781422237281 (hardback: alk. paper) | ISBN 9781422280614 (ebook)
Subjects: LCSH: Phobias in children—Juvenile literature.
Classification: LCC RJ506.P38 P66 2018 (print) | LCC RJ506.P38 (ebook) | DDC
    618.92/85225—dc23
LC record available at https://lccn.loc.gov/2016053122

Printed and bound in the United States of America.

First printing
9 8 7 6 5 4 3 2 1

TABLE OF CONTENTS

Key Icons to Look for:

 Words to Understand: These words with their easy-to-understand definitions will increase the reader's understanding of the text, while building vocabulary skills.

 Sidebars: This boxed material within the main text allows readers to build knowledge, gain insights, explore possibilities, and broaden their perspectives by weaving together additional information to provide realistic and holistic perspectives.

 Educational Videos: Readers can view videos by scanning our QR codes, which will provide them with additional educational content to supplement the text. Examples include news coverage, moments in history, speeches, iconic sports moments, and much more.

 Text-Dependent Questions: These questions send the reader back to the text for more careful attention to the evidence presented there.

 Research Projects: Readers are pointed toward areas of further inquiry connected to each chapter. Suggestions are provided for projects that encourage deeper research and analysis.

 Series Glossary of Key Terms: This back-of-the-book glossary contains terminology used throughout the series. Words found here increase the reader's ability to read and comprehend higher-level books and articles in this field.

SERIES INTRODUCTION

Who among us does not have memories of an intense childhood fear? Fears and anxieties are a part of *every* childhood. Indeed, these fears are fodder for urban legends and campfire tales alike. And while the details of these legends and tales change over time, they generally have at their base predictable childhood terrors such as darkness, separation from caretakers, or bodily injury.

We know that fear has an evolutionary component. Infants are helpless, and, compared to other mammals, humans have a very long developmental period. Fear ensures that curious children will stay close to caretakers, making them less likely to be exposed to danger. This means that childhood fears are adaptive, making us more likely to survive, and even thrive, as a species.

Unfortunately, there comes a point when fear and anxiety cease to be useful. This is especially problematic today, for there has been a startling increase in anxiety among children and adolescents. In fact, 25 percent of 13- to 18-year-olds now have mild to moderate anxiety, and the *median* age of onset for anxiety disorders is just 11 years old.

Why might this be? Some say that the contemporary United States is a nation preoccupied with risk, and it is certainly possible that our children are absorbing this preoccupation as well. Certainly, our exposure to potential threats has never been greater. We see graphic images via the media and have more immediate news of all forms of disaster. This can lead our children to feel more vulnerable, and it may increase the likelihood that they respond with fear. If children based their fear on the news that they see on Facebook or on TV, they would dramatically overestimate the likelihood of terrible things happening.

As parents or teachers, what do we do about fear? As in other areas of life, we provide our children with guidance and education on a daily basis. We teach them about the signs and feelings of fear. We discuss and normalize typical fear reactions, and support them in tackling difficult situations despite fear. We explain—and demonstrate by example—how to identify "negative thinking traps" and generate positive coping thoughts instead.

But to do so effectively, we might need to challenge some of our own assumptions about fear. Adults often assume that they must protect their children from fear and help them to avoid scary situations, when sometimes the best course is for the child to face the fear and conquer it. This is counterintuitive for many adults: after all, isn't it our job to reassure our children and help them feel better? Yes, of course! Except when it isn't. Sometimes they need us to help them confront their fears and move forward anyway.

That's where these volumes come in. When it comes to fear, balanced information is critical. Learning about fear as it relates to many different areas can help us to help our children remember that although you don't choose whether to be afraid, you do choose how to handle it. These volumes explore the world of childhood fears, seeking to answer important questions: How much is too much? And how can fear be positive, functioning to mobilize us in the face of danger?

Fear gives us the opportunity to step up and respond with courage and resilience. It pushes us to expand our sphere of functioning to areas that might feel unfamiliar or risky. When we are a little nervous or afraid, we tend to prepare a little more, look for more information, ask more questions—and all of this can function to help us expand the boundaries of our lives in a positive direction. So, while fear might *feel* unpleasant, there is no doubt that it can have a positive outcome.

Let's teach our children that.

—Anne Walters, Ph.D.
Chief Psychologist, Emma Pendleton Bradley Hospital
Clinical Associate Professor,
Alpert Medical School of Brown University

Claustrophobia is the fear of confined or crowded spaces.

CHAPTER ONE

WHAT ARE PHOBIAS?

You have probably heard people say they have "a phobia" about something. It might be heights. Or spiders. Even clowns.

What people mean by phobia, in most cases, is that they are very bothered by that particular thing. For example, if someone says, "I have a phobia about crowds," that person usually means that being in a large group of people makes him or her feel anxious and uncomfortable. The person is saying she or he would rather avoid a crowd if possible.

For casual, everyday speech, that is a pretty good definition. But in medicine, the word *phobia* has a much more specific meaning. In this book, we'll look at the medical version of the word, especially as it relates to kids. Then we'll look at how phobias are treated, and what you can do to try to overcome whatever phobias you might have.

 **WORDS TO UNDERSTAND**

criteria: a set of standards by which you can judge something.

genetic: here, describing a trait that is passed along in families.

panic attack: sudden episode of intense, overwhelming fear.

proportion: a part of something as compared to the whole.

stimulus: something that causes a particular reaction.

SPECIFIC PHOBIA

Doctors have identified a medical condition called "specific phobia." This is similar to our casual idea of phobias, but there are particular criteria that have to be met. People with a specific phobia will have the following symptoms:

- They feel intense fear or anxiety.
- They fear a particular thing or situation.
- This fear is out of proportion to the actual threat.
- They feel this fear or anxiety to a degree that negatively impacts daily life.

Let's look at each of those four aspects in turn. First, consider the intensity of the fear. Someone with a specific phobia does not just feel vaguely uncomfortable. People with specific phobia have real physical symptoms, such as sweating, pounding heart, difficulty breathing, dizziness, and trembling or shaking. Sometimes people with specific phobias have panic attacks.

Next, the fear must relate to a particular thing or situation. a true medical phobia requires what doctors call a *phobic stimulus*. That's a fancy term for the specific thing that makes you afraid. A specific phobia is different from anxiety in general. Some people feel anxious about all kinds of things, or, in the case of anxiety disorder, they feel anxious for no reason at all. That is definitely a problem, but it is not a specific phobia.

EDUCATIONAL VIDEO

Watch this video for more information on types of phobias.

Whatever it is that sparks your fear is called a *phobic stimulus*. People with trypophobia have a fear of certain types of holes; for them, a sponge may be a phobic stimulus.

Third, the issue of proportion is really important. Let's say you are camping in the woods. In the morning, you put on your boot, only to find that a snake crawled into it during the night. You might freak out a little bit, and nobody would blame you; fear is a reasonable response to the situation. But if you are *constantly* afraid of snakes—if you freak out about seeing a snake on TV, for example— that's different. A snake on TV can't possibly hurt you, which means that your fear would be out of proportion to the threat.

Finally, the fear must be so intense that it has a negative impact on life. Let's say that someone says she has a phobia of enclosed spaces like elevators. Her doctor will want to know what she does whenever she has to get to a high floor in a building. If she takes the elevator even though she

ONE OR MORE

Three-quarters of the people who have phobias have more than one. In other words, if a person has a specific phobia about enclosed spaces, it is more likely that he or she will also have a phobia about flying.

hates it, she probably does not have a phobia in the medical sense. Her fear of elevators is bothersome, but it doesn't actually stop her from doing what she needs to do. But if she refuses to go in the building all, that's different. Or maybe she takes the stairs and climbs 30 flights—ending up sweaty, exhausted, and late for her appointment. If she will do pretty much anything to avoid that elevator, that may be a true phobia.

CAUSES

Sometimes people have a bad experience and then develop a phobia related to it. Take the story about finding a snake in your boot. Your initial fear made sense: there was an actual snake in your actual boot. But if you start feeling afraid of *all* snakes, you may have *ophidiophobia,* or the extreme, irrational fear of snakes.

Sometimes witnessing a scary thing is enough to kick off a phobia. For instance, your camping buddy might say, "One time my friend found a snake in his boot, and I've been terrified of snakes ever since!" Other times, the media is

Opposite: About 10 percent of Americans have acrophobia, which is the unreasonable fear of heights. People with acrophobia may also fear falling, even when they are not high up.

partly to blame—if the news talks constantly about snakebites, some people might find their ophidiophobia getting worse.

But it's a strange thing: cowboys have been finding snakes in their boots for a long time, but they don't all have ophidiophobia. They just laugh it off (and probably kill the snake). So what makes one person able to laugh something off, while another can't? We don't really know.

It does seem possible that there may be a genetic cause, meaning some people are naturally more anxious than others, and that gets passed down to their kids. The extreme fear of needles is

It's not uncommon to be afraid of a snake that could hurt you. But if you truly have ophidiophobia, your fear is way out of proportion to the actual threat.

UNUSUAL PHOBIAS

People seem to love making up phobia names. There are hundreds of names for different types of fears. Some might not qualify as true medical phobias—remember, true specific phobias need to meet the criteria mentioned in the text. But keep in mind, even if it sounds strange to you, it can be serious to the person who has it.

Do you or does anyone you know have any of these phobias?

- barophobia: fear of gravity.
- geliophobia: fear of laughter.
- globophobia: fear of balloons.
- hexakosioihexekontahexaphobia: fear of the number 666.
- lutraphobia: fear of otters.
- pedophobia: fear of children.
- phobophobia: fear of phobias.
- pteronophobia: fear of being tickled by feathers.
- vestiphobia: fear of clothes.

particularly common in families. It's also possible that phobias are learned; in other words, if you see your parents acting afraid, you might learn to be afraid, too.

The truth is, *why* people fear the things they do is a bit of a mystery! But even if motives are hard to figure out, we do know a lot about behavior, or the actions people take in response to fear. And the number one type of behavior in people with phobias is to stay as far away from the scary thing as possible.

ANTICIPATION AND AVOIDANCE

One thing that makes phobias so challenging is that the fear can crop up even when the person isn't near the thing that frightens them. This is called *anticipatory anxiety.* For someone with a medical phobia, for example, just making an appointment is a very scary concept. If someone has this type of phobia, even *thinking* about going to the doctor can be upsetting.

A common reaction to anticipatory anxiety is to avoid the frightening thing as much as possible. Actions we take to steer clear of our phobias are called *avoidance behaviors*. For example, if you have *cynophobia*, which is the fear of dogs, you would probably not walk down a particular street where the people have dogs. Or if a friend has a dog, you might refuse to go to his house. You might avoid going to the park on a Saturday because so many people bring dogs there. Those are avoidance behaviors, and they have a negative impact on your life because they limit the places you can go and the things you're able to do.

How much a phobia affects your life depends a lot on the phobic stimulus. For instance, the problems caused by a dog phobia are minor compared to a person with, for example, *iatrophobia*, or an intense fear of doctors. Avoiding a friend who has a dog might upset

the friend, but avoiding doctors, even when you badly need one, can be extremely dangerous. An extreme fear of school (*didaskaleinophobia,* but often just called "school phobia") can have a destructive effect on a person's future. (In fact, there is an another book in this set, *School Fears,* entirely devoted to this issue.)

If you have an intense fear of dogs, just thinking about walking by a house where a dog lives might bring on your phobia.

 TEXT-DEPENDENT QUESTIONS

1. What are the four criteria that define a true phobia?

2. What is a phobic stimulus?

3. What's the term for being afraid of something before it even happens?

Agoraphobia can
leave people feeling
isolated.

CHAPTER TWO

TWO SPECIAL CASES

Many phobias are fairly straightforward, and the cause of these phobias is easy to figure out. A person with arachnophobia fears spiders, while a person with acrophobia fears heights. But there are two types of phobias that are a bit more complex: agoraphobia and social phobia (also called social anxiety). Perhaps it's because both of them involve our interactions with others—and people, as we know, are complicated.

AGORAPHOBIA

In ancient Greece, every city had a central gathering place called the *agora*. There was usually a marketplace, and at least one temple. Essentially, the agora was the heart of the city, so avoiding the agora would mean avoiding life itself. Today, the agora gives its name to a very particular type of fear: agoraphobia, or the intense fear of public spaces.

WORDS TO UNDERSTAND

comorbid: when one illness or disorder is present alongside another one.

diagnose: to identify an illness or disorder.

enclosed: surrounded or closed in.

self-conscious: overly aware of yourself, to the point that it makes you awkward.

stereotype: an oversimplified idea about a type of person that may not be true for any given individual.

The agora in Smyrna (now part of Turkey) was the center of life in the ancient Greek city. It is now an open-air museum.

If someone has an extreme case of agoraphobia, he or she never leaves home—or certainly not willingly. That is the stereotype of agoraphobics that we see in movies and on TV. But the condition of agoraphobia can actually look different in different people. Not all people with agoraphobia are unwilling to leave their homes.

Mental health professionals use a book called the *Diagnostic and Statistical Manual of Mental Disorders* (*DSM*) to diagnose patients. The symptoms of agoraphobia are the same as the ones listed in chapter one. But the DSM states that a person must experience those symptoms in at least two of these five situations:

- when using public transportation (could be buses, trains, planes, etc.);
- in open spaces (could be a field, a bridge, or other);

- in enclosed spaces (like a supermarket, a movie theater, or other);
- in a crowd or a line of people;
- alone outside of one's home.

Note that agoraphobia does not necessarily mean that the person is afraid to go out at all, although it can mean that. The fears of someone with agoraphobia are better described as being afraid of places that feel unsafe to them.

One challenging thing about agoraphobia is that the symptoms can look like something else. For example, an intense fear of flying may in fact be agoraphobia in disguise. It depends on whether the person has *other* fears as well, or if it is only the plane that bothers them. A condition

Agoraphobia sometimes goes hand-in-hand with depression; other times, one condition is confused with the other.

CLAUSTROPHOBIA

A common phobia that is easily mixed up with agoraphobia is one called *claustrophobia*. In Latin, *claustrum* is a "shut-in place," and claustrophobia refers to the extreme fear of being in an enclosed space with no escape. Elevators are notoriously difficult for people with claustrophobia. Some people with agoraphobia may also have trouble in elevators and enclosed spaces. But people with agoraphobia are likely to have just as much trouble with a wide-open but crowded space—something that would not trouble someone with claustrophobia.

Claustrophobia can bring on panic attacks.

called claustrophobia can also be confused with agoraphobia (see box).

Depression is another disorder that can complicate the situation. Someone who is suffering from depression may not want to go out. When you're depressed, you may not have any energy for your friends. In that case, the last thing you want is to deal with strangers at a busy shopping mall or restaurant. But this doesn't mean that you have agoraphobia. The symptoms of depression may *look* a bit like agoraphobia, but the causes (and treatments) are quite different.

People who have agoraphobia frequently do have other mental conditions as well. Doctors say that agoraphobia is often comorbid with other problems, including depression, panic disorder, and additional specific phobias, especially social phobia. Agoraphobia is very difficult to cure completely, but with treatment the symptoms can get a lot better. (See chapter four for more information on treatments.)

SOCIAL PHOBIA

Agoraphobia has to do with a fear of unsafe spaces— or rather, spaces that the person *believes* are unsafe, even if that's not true. Social phobia has to do with the fear that other people are unsafe. Social phobia is more commonly called *social anxiety disorder.*

People with this disorder often assume that they will be horribly embarrassed at any moment, and they will do anything to keep that from happening. They are intensely self-conscious and afraid of being judged by others. Some people with social phobias only worry about having to "perform" in front of others, such as when they have to give a presentation at school. Other people focus more on social interactions, like meeting someone new, talking to authority figures, or eating in public.

EDUCATIONAL VIDEO

Check out this video about agoraphobia.

Class presentations can be extremely difficult for people with social phobia.

EDUCATIONAL VIDEO

Here's a video on the difference between shyness and social phobia.

People with social anxiety disorder do everything they can to avoid these types of situations. On top of that, they constantly worry that the situation might happen anyway. If they are forced into a social interaction they are not ready for, they tend to panic, experiencing physical symptoms like sweating, shaking, nausea, and dizziness.

Every single person has felt shy at times. Every person has worried at some point about what other people think about him or her. Having these feelings from time to time does not mean you have social phobia—it means you are human. But sometimes these fears start to take over a person's life. If you find that you are not doing things you would like to do because fear is holding you back, then that could be the beginning of social phobia. If being forced to speak in class makes you feel sick, that also is probably above and beyond "typical" social fears.

About 75 percent of people with social anxiety started to experience the symptoms between the ages of 8 and 13. Because it's so common in young people, there is an entire other book about it in this set, called *Social Fears*.

 **RESEARCH PROJECT**

Write a biography of a famous person with agoraphobia, such as Emily Dickinson (poet), Howard Hughes (businessman), Edvard Munch (painter), or Brian Wilson (musician). You can also find other examples. Consider how the disorder impacted their lives.

 TEXT-DEPENDENT QUESTIONS

1. Where does the name *agoraphobia* come from?

2. What kinds of situations would be avoided by someone with agoraphobia?

3. How is social phobia different from shyness?

Clowns are supposed to be fun for kids, but a lot of young people find them scary.

CHAPTER THREE

KIDS AND PHOBIAS

Most phobias begin in childhood. Frequently, something happens in a kid's life, and he or she develops a phobia related to that event. If the phobia isn't treated or addressed, it may continue to bother the person well into adulthood.

Being bitten by a dog is a common example of a traumatic event that can turn into a phobia. Sometimes the event is not quite that dramatic, however. For example, seeing a photo of a scary clown can plant a seed in the back of someone's mind. Years later, the person might find all clowns to be scary, but not remember the photo that first started it. In fact, many adults can't remember when or why they developed a specific phobia; they just know they have had it for a long time.

A person can have a phobia at any age. But some aspects of phobias are a bit different for kids than for adults.

WORDS TO UNDERSTAND

phases: stages of development.

reluctance: unwillingness.

vulnerable: defenseless.

JUST A PHASE?

Fears are a part of normal life, and that is doubly true when it comes to children. Many of our fears are caused by the unknown, and there's just a lot that kids don't know yet! Another factor that makes us more fearful is our imaginations, and kids tend to have better imaginations than most adults. That mix—not knowing certain things but imagining *lots* of things— makes kids especially vulnerable to phobias.

But there is an upside, which is that kids often grow out of their phobias. As you get older and have more experiences, you tend to realize that things that seemed very scary are actually not such a big deal. Fear of the dark is a great example; when you were

Nighttime can be scary for little kids with active imaginations.

TYPICAL CHILDHOOD PHOBIAS

These are just a few of the most common things kids have phobias about:

- spiders, bees, and other insects
- needles and blood
- dentists and doctors

- loud noises
- crowds
- dogs or other large animals

What would you add to this list?

three or four years old, the idea of a monster in your room might have seemed totally reasonable (and scary!). Just a few years later, that probably seemed pretty silly. Another way to say this is that kids go through **phases**: they are afraid of certain things for a while, and then they stop feeling that way.

At least that's how childhood fears are supposed to work. But life doesn't always go the way it is supposed to. Sometimes we don't outgrow our fears. Unfortunately, sometimes they just get worse. Figuring out whether a specific fear is a phase or a problem can be tricky. Doctors look for the kinds of symptoms listed in chapter one. They also consider how long the person has had the fear and how much the fear gets in the way of daily life.

UNAVOIDABLE?

Another thing doctors look for is the avoidance behavior discussed in chapter one. But avoidance

Kids don't have the power to avoid their phobias the way many adults do.

behavior is more complicated for kids than it is for adults. And it's pretty easy to understand why: kids aren't in charge!

An adult can decide whether or not to make a doctor's appointment, and later he can decide whether or not to go. An adult can say, "Nope, I don't want that medical procedure." But if you're a kid, an adult makes the appointment and then makes sure you show up for it. If the doctor says it's time for a procedure, chances are it's going to happen whether you like it or not.

Kids can't necessarily "avoid" a phobic stimulus the way an adult does. And if kids can't avoid their phobia in a calm way, they might be *less calm* about it. Kids with phobias tend to have tantrums. They might cry, scream, or run away and hide. This "acting out," as adults like to say, is the result of their lack of control over their world.

When kids throw tantrums—especially when they are school-aged kids who seem "too old" for that sort of thing—adults may react very badly. But rather than simply punishing the bad behavior, it's important for adults to try and understand what's causing it. If you are a kid and you sometimes lose control in the face of something scary, it's a good idea to talk to an adult about it. Not when the scary thing is happening—you may be too upset to explain yourself at that time. But later, when you feel calm and can express yourself better, let an adult know about your fears. Talking about your fears is the first step toward beating them (see chapter four for more about this).

SOUND OF SILENCE

While some kids with phobias "act out" when they are afraid, others have the opposite reaction: they keep everything inside.

There is nothing wrong with being a quiet sort of person. But someone who is afraid to speak can have a lot of problems. For example, a kid who is

EDUCATIONAL VIDEO

Check out this video on selective mutism.

Selective mutism usually begins when kids are around five or six years old.

afraid of teachers might not tell anyone if he gets hurt on the playground. Sometimes this reluctance to speak gets so bad that kids barely speak at all. If you try and talk to them, they won't answer. They might just stare at you, or they might turn their heads or even run away.

You might think a kid like that is weird or doesn't have any emotions. But it's likely that he or she actually has a very challenging type of anxiety called *selective mutism*. The word *mute* means that the person doesn't speak; *selective* refers to the fact that the person *could* speak (there is nothing physically wrong) but doesn't. Oftentimes, kids with selective mutism are able to speak when they are at home, but are too scared to do it anywhere

else. Unfortunately, sometimes parents interpret this silence as evidence that their child is being "difficult" on purpose. But kids with selective mutism are almost never doing it on purpose. They may want to speak very much, but they just feel like it's an impossible task.

Selective mutism usually starts when a child is around five years old, which is about the time most kids start kindergarten. It usually goes hand-in-hand with other anxiety problems—about 90 percent of kids with selective mutism also have social phobia. Because of that, selective mutism is usually treated alongside those other anxiety problems. (See chapter two for an explanation of social phobia, and chapter four for treatment information.)

RESEARCH PROJECT

Choose a phobia from the list on page 15, or choose another. Find out what causes it, who tends to have it, and what can be done. Write up a short guide that a person could use to start overcoming the phobia. (Be sure to check out the explanation of exposure therapy in chapter four!)

TEXT-DEPENDENT QUESTIONS

1. Why might phobia symptoms look different in kids than adults?

2. What are some typical childhood phobias?

3. What is selective mutism?

It can be helpful to talk about your fears with an adult you trust.

CHAPTER FOUR

FACING PHOBIAS

The first step in overcoming any problem is figuring out the cause. Sometimes it's pretty easy. For instance, if you have an intense fear of dogs, that will be obvious. You're not afraid of cats or guinea pigs, just dogs. But in other cases, the specific cause of the fear—the actual phobic stimulus—is not as clear-cut.

NAMING THE FEARS

One of the most challenging phobias for kids is school phobia. But school has a lot of different components—before you can address the phobia, you need to figure out which aspects of school are really the problem. Is it other kids? Is it academic stress? Those are two different types of problems, and they need different solutions. Or maybe it's really the crowds of kids at school that are bothering you, rather than the school itself. Maybe you are afraid of a terrible event like a shooting, or maybe

WORDS TO UNDERSTAND

components: parts.

evaluated: examined.

exposure: having contact with something.

sedative: a type of drug that slows down bodily processes, making people feel relaxed or even sleepy.

you are afraid of leaving home because you are worried about your parents for some reason. All kinds of different fears could be buried beneath the surface.

It's important to figure out the true source of the anxiety. It may be helpful to talk through your fears with an adult. If you feel comfortable talking to your parent or guardian about these issues, that is definitely the best place to start. A teacher, school counselor, pediatrician, or church leader are also good options.

GETTING HELP

Milder phobias can sometimes be faced on your own. But when it comes to big phobias—like if you are too afraid to go to school or to even leave your house—getting help from someone in the mental health field is probably necessary.

It can be tricky to figure out whether treatment is needed or not. It's true, sometimes kids do outgrow their fears. But sometimes that doesn't happen. Other times the damage being done by the phobia (due to missing school, for instance) is so great that the fear can't be left untreated. That's why it's important to be **evaluated** by a professional. Doctors are often in a better position to determine whether a phobia is something that needs treatment. In fact, phobias are a major reason why kids go to therapy.

PHOBIAS AND POLITICS

Phobias are so much a part of our culture that they even come up in political discussions. You might have heard someone described as *homophobic*. Technically, this means the unreasonable fear of people who are gay or lesbian. In practice, however, the term describes beliefs, behavior, or policies that are damaging to people in the LGBT community. In other words, homophobia doesn't usually mean that someone is literally *afraid* of gay people, but rather that the person discriminates against them.

Another important political phobia is *xenophobia*. Xenophobia is the fear of foreigners or outsiders. Again, people who are xenophobic aren't necessarily "afraid" of foreigners, but rather are hostile to them.

A protest against xenophobia in 2016.

Psychiatrists, psychologists, social workers, and counselors are specially trained to help people overcome fears. What type of treatment is needed depends on a few factors, including the type of phobia, the kinds of avoidance behaviors involved, and how intensely the phobia hurts the person's life.

TYPES OF TREATMENT

Have you ever gone swimming in cold water, like the ocean or a lake? One way people deal with cold water is to go in very slowly, one step at a time. Maybe they just get their feet first. Then when their feet don't feel so cold, they take another step into the water. Then when they get used to it, they take another step, and so on. Exposure therapy works basically like that.

Let's say that someone has a severe phobia of dogs. The therapist might first just talk with the person about dogs. When talking about dogs feels okay, the person might look at a picture of a dog. When pictures are no longer scary, maybe the person would watch videos about dogs. Over time, the person would "work up" to being in a room with a real dog. In the same way that people get used to cold water a little at a time, people with phobias can learn that they have nothing to fear. Exposure therapy takes patience, but it is very effective if done correctly. One study showed that as many as 90 percent of adults with phobias show improvement after exposure therapy.

Sometimes people with phobias need more help, though. There is no pill that can make phobias disappear, but doctors sometimes prescribe medications that help people feel more calm. A common example involves the fear of flying. Doctors sometimes give adults a sedative to take right

Opposite: If a phobia interferes with daily life, it may be time to get help from an expert.

WORRYING ABOUT WORRYING

One very difficult problem for people with phobias is the anticipatory anxiety we discussed in chapter one. Let's say that someone with claustrophobia is forced, for whatever reason, to take an elevator. There's just no way to avoid it. Once on the elevator, the person starts to panic: her heart races, she sweats and trembles . . . it's a panic attack.

Now, that's definitely bad. But both the elevator ride and the panic attack will end eventually. The bigger problem starts later, when she remembers the experience. Sometimes people have new panic attacks just thinking about the panic attack they had before. The memory of the panic attack and the fear that it will return can be worse than the initial incident.

This is why exposure therapy can be so helpful. By easing someone

into the situation a tiny bit at a time, the person can slowly gain confidence. Every time the person gets a bit closer to the scary situation and does *not* have a panic attack, that's a big victory. Exposure therapy is a way to break the cycle of worrying about worrying.

One of the toughest parts of dealing with phobias is anticipatory anxiety, or worrying about how you might be scared later.

before a flight. Sedatives can be addictive, however, so this has to be done carefully.

People with agoraphobia or social phobia (both discussed in chapter two) may be given antidepressants. These medications affect the parts of the brain that control mood. Antidepressants aren't magic; they don't make people *un*afraid all of a sudden. Instead, the medications help people begin to think differently about their fears.

Beta-blockers are another type of medication that can be helpful in certain situations. These drugs reduce the physical reactions to phobias, such as a racing heart, elevated blood pressure, or shaky limbs. Studies have shown that beta-blockers reduce or even eliminate the extreme fear of people with phobias. What is not clear, however, is how long the effect lasts. Although an easy cure to phobias would be great, right now it seems like medicine can only help in the short term. So far, there is no substitute for someone learning to overcome a phobia.

TIPS FOR FACING PHOBIAS

Here are some ways you can face a phobia:

- **Practice relaxation.** Notice how your body reacts to discomfort and try to relax. If your jaw is clenched, make a point of releasing it. If your fists have suddenly clenched up, open them. Pause for a moment to focus on your breathing: take a deep, slow breath in through

EDUCATIONAL VIDEO

Check out this video for more advice about overcoming phobias.

RESEARCH PROJECT

RESEARCH PROJECT

Choose a small fear to overcome, like saying hello to a stranger, overcoming a fear of spiders, or sleeping without a night-light. Use exposure therapy techniques to try and get used to the thing you fear. Check out The Psych Show's demonstration of exposure therapy (https://youtu.be/2z-ZGt_vD5A) and follow the steps. If possible, do this with a buddy so you can support each other. Keep a journal about your experience.

your nose, hold it for a few seconds, and then breathe out slowly through your mouth. Do this a few times in a row. It might sound strange, but it works.

- **Write, draw, or think about your fears.** When you are in the middle of the situation, it can be hard to see it clearly. If you analyze it later, however, when you are feeling safe, you might see things differently. Try writing about what makes you afraid (or draw it, if that's more your thing). Picture yourself in the situation that bothers you. What exactly is making you uncomfortable? Answer honestly: is there a real threat, or is it mainly in your imagination? You may realize that what you thought was big and scary is not so big at all.

- **Try the 20-second strategy.** First, count slowly from 1 to 20. That's roughly 20 seconds. Not long at all, right? You can do pretty much anything for 20 seconds. When you have a phobia, it's easy to start thinking that the scared feeling is going to last forever. But it won't! If you focus on getting through 20 seconds at a time, you'll be amazed how far you can go.

- **Tell a friend.** The truth is, everybody is afraid of something. Talk to a friend or an adult you trust about your fear, and ask him or her to

back you up as you face it. Maybe that person also has a fear, and the two of you can stand up to your phobias together. Don't try to beat your fears alone.

Sharing your worries with friends can make you realize that you aren't alone.

 TEXT-DEPENDENT QUESTIONS

1. When is it important to be evaluated by a mental health professional?

2. What is exposure therapy?

3. What are some other things people can try to overcome their fears?

FURTHER READING

Anxiety and Depression Association of America. "Specific Phobias." December 2015. https://www.adaa.org/understanding-anxiety/specific-phobias.

Bourne, Edmund. *The Anxiety and Phobia Workbook.* 6th ed. Oakland, CA: New Harbinger, 2015.

Gallo, Donald R. *What Are You Afraid Of? Stories about Phobias.* Cambridge, MA: Candlewick, 2006.

KidsHealth. "Phobias." http://kidshealth.org/en/kids/phobias.html

Latta, Sara. *Scared Stiff: Everything You Need to Know About 50 Famous Phobias.* San Francisco, CA: Zest Books, 2013.

EDUCATIONAL VIDEOS

Chapter One: Osmosis. "Phobias—Specific Phobias, Agoraphobia, and Social Phobia." https://youtu.be/PCOg2G797ek.

Chapter Two: Kati Morton. "What Is Agoraphobia?" https://youtu.be/VrKfNlLalPs.

Chapter Two: Stuff Mom Never Told You. "Shy vs. Social Anxiety." https://youtu.be/We6U-KrJ6E4.

Chapter Three: ABC News. "Curing Kids with Extreme Social Phobias." https://youtu.be/i7EAsMNZ6uA.

Chapter Four: The Psych Show. "How to Use Exposure Therapy to Overcome Phobias." https://youtu.be/2z-ZGt_vD5A.

SERIES GLOSSARY

adaptive: a helpful response to a particular situation.

bias: a feeling against a particular thing or idea.

biofeedback: monitoring of bodily functions with the goal of learning to control those functions.

cognitive: relating to the brain and thought.

comorbid: when one illness or disorder is present alongside another one.

context: the larger situation in which an event takes place.

diagnose: to identify an illness or disorder.

exposure: having contact with something.

extrovert: a person who enjoys being with others.

harassment: picking on another person frequently and deliberately.

hypnosis: creating a state of consciousness where someone is awake but highly open to suggestion.

inhibitions: feelings that restricts what we do or say.

introvert: a person who prefers being alone.

irrational: baseless; something that's not connected to reality.

melatonin: a substance that helps the body regulate sleep.

milestone: an event that marks a stage in development.

motivating: something that makes you want to work harder.

occasional: from time to time; not often.

panic attack: sudden episode of intense, overwhelming fear.

paralyzing: something that makes you unable to move (can refer to physical movement as well as emotions).

peers: people who are roughly the same age as you.

perception: what we see and believe to be true.

persistent: continuing for a noticeable period.

phobia: extreme fear of a particular thing.

preventive: keeping something from happening.

probability: the likelihood that a particular thing will happen.

psychological: having to do with the mind and thoughts.

rational: based on a calm understanding of facts, rather than emotion.

sedative: a type of drug that slows down bodily processes, making people feel relaxed or even sleepy.

self-conscious: overly aware of yourself, to the point that it makes you awkward.

serotonin: a chemical in the brain that is important in moods.

stereotype: an oversimplified idea about a type of person that may not be true for any given individual.

stigma: a sense of shame or disgrace associated with a particular state of being.

stimulant: a group of substances that speed up bodily processes.

subconscious: thoughts and feelings you have but may not be aware of.

syndrome: a condition.

treatable: describes a medical condition that can be healed.

upheaval: a period of great change or uncertainty.

INDEX

ABOUT THE ADVISOR

Anne S. Walters is Clinical Associate Professor of Psychiatry and Human Behavior at the Alpert Medical School of Brown University. She is also Chief Psychologist for Bradley Hospital. She is actively involved in teaching activities within the Clinical Psychology Training Programs of the Alpert Medical School and serves as Child Track Seminar Co-Coordinator. Dr. Walters completed her undergraduate work at Duke University, graduate school at Georgia State University, internship at UTexas Health Science Center, and postdoctoral fellowship at Brown University.

ABOUT THE AUTHOR

H. W. Poole is a writer and editor of books for young people, including the sets, *Families Today* and *Mental Illnesses and Disorders: Awareness and Understanding* (Mason Crest). She created the *Horrors of History* series (Charlesbridge) and the *Ecosystems* series (Facts On File). She has also been responsible for many critically acclaimed reference books, including *Political Handbook of the World* (CQ Press) and the *Encyclopedia of Terrorism* (SAGE). She was coauthor and editor of *The History of the Internet* (ABC-CLIO), which won the 2000 American Library Association RUSA award.

PHOTO CREDITS